A TASTE OF HOME
Christmas Cookies

**RECIPES COOKBOOK &
CHRISTMAS COOKIES
COLORING BOOK in one!**

Copyright © 2020 by Inspire Studios

New England Christmas Cookies

3/4 cup of melted shortening
3/4 cup of melted butter
1 cup of brown sugar
1 cup of white sugar
1 teaspoon of cinnamon
1 cup of sliced blanched almonds
3 eggs, beaten
1 teaspoon of salt
3 1/2 cups of flour
1 1/2 teaspoons of soda

Cream sugar and melted ingredients.
Beat eggs and add to creamed mixture.
Sift together all dry ingredients and
beat into dough.
Stir in almonds.
Form dough into small rolls and
wrap in wax paper.
Refrigerate overnight.
Slice thin and bake at 350 degrees
for 8 to 10 minutes.
DO NOT OVERBAKE.

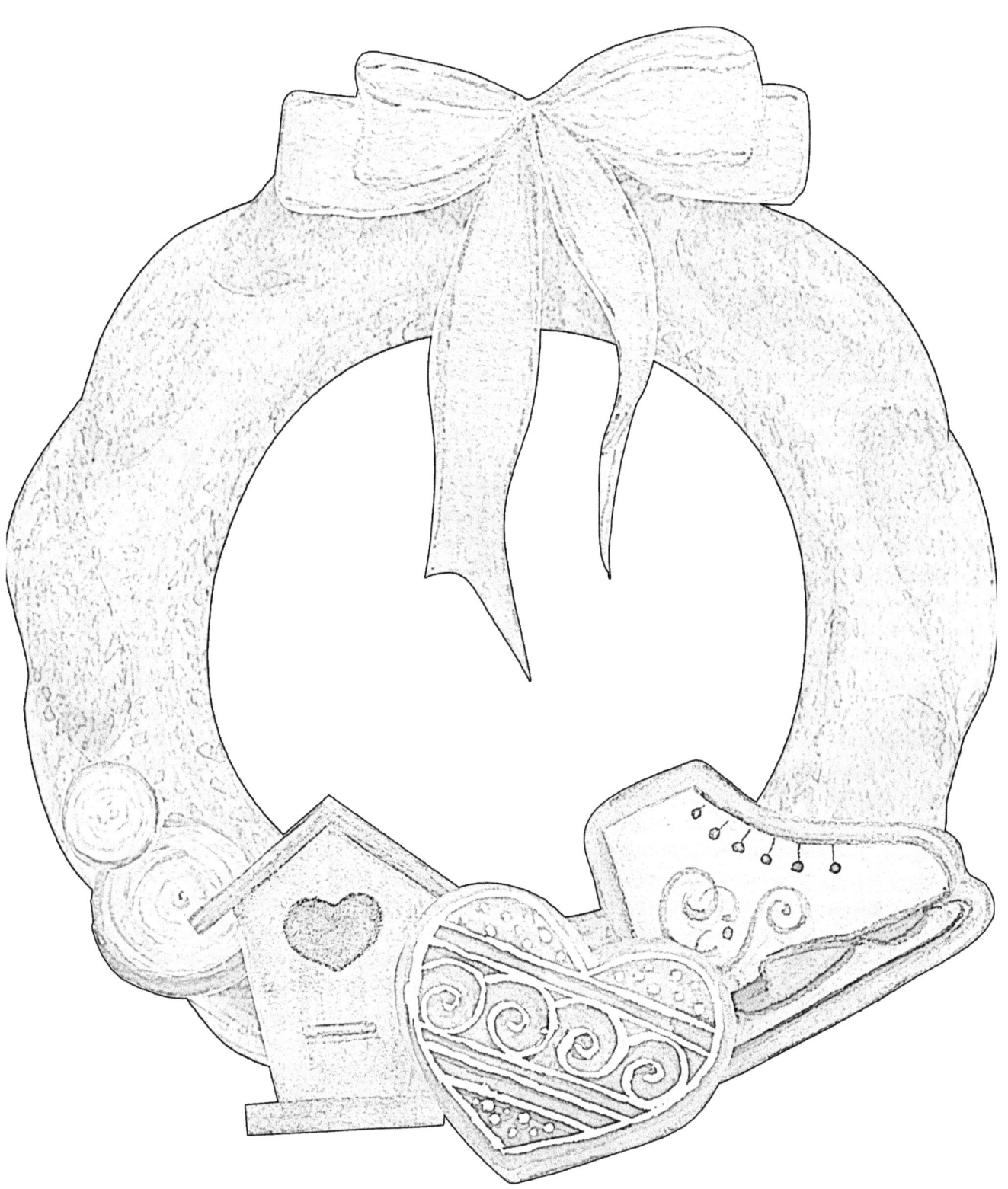

Chocolate Covered Cherry Cookies

1 1/2 cups of all-purpose flour
1/2 cup of unsweetened cocoa powder
1/4 teaspoon of salt
1/4 teaspoon of baking soda
1/4 teaspoon of baking powder
1/2 cup of butter or margarine softened
1 cup of granulated sugar
1 egg
1 1/2 teaspoons of vanilla
1 -10 ounce jar of maraschino cherries, drained, reserve juice
1 - 6 ounce package of semisweet chocolate chips
1/2 cup of sweetened condensed milk

In large bowl, stir together flour, cocoa powder, salt, baking powder and soda. In mixer bowl, beat together butter or margarine and sugar on low speed until fluffy. Add egg and vanilla; beat well. Gradually add dry ingredients to creamed mixture; beat until well

Christmas Cookie Wreaths

2 eggs, beaten
1/2 cup of butter
1 cup of chopped raisins
1 teaspoon of vanilla extract
1/2 teaspoon of ground ginger
1 cup of sugar
4 teaspoons of sweet cream
1 teaspoon of baking soda
1 teaspoon of ground cinnamon
3 1/2 cups of flour (sifted)

Mix butter and sugar in bowl until creamy. Whip eggs and sweet cream. Add other ingredients and mix well until mixture becomes dough. Place in refrigerator to chill. Preheat oven to 375 degrees. Remove dough from refrigerator and cut small pieces. Roll into wreath shapes. Place on ungreased cookie sheet. Bake for 12 minutes. Let cookies cool. Add decorations if desired.

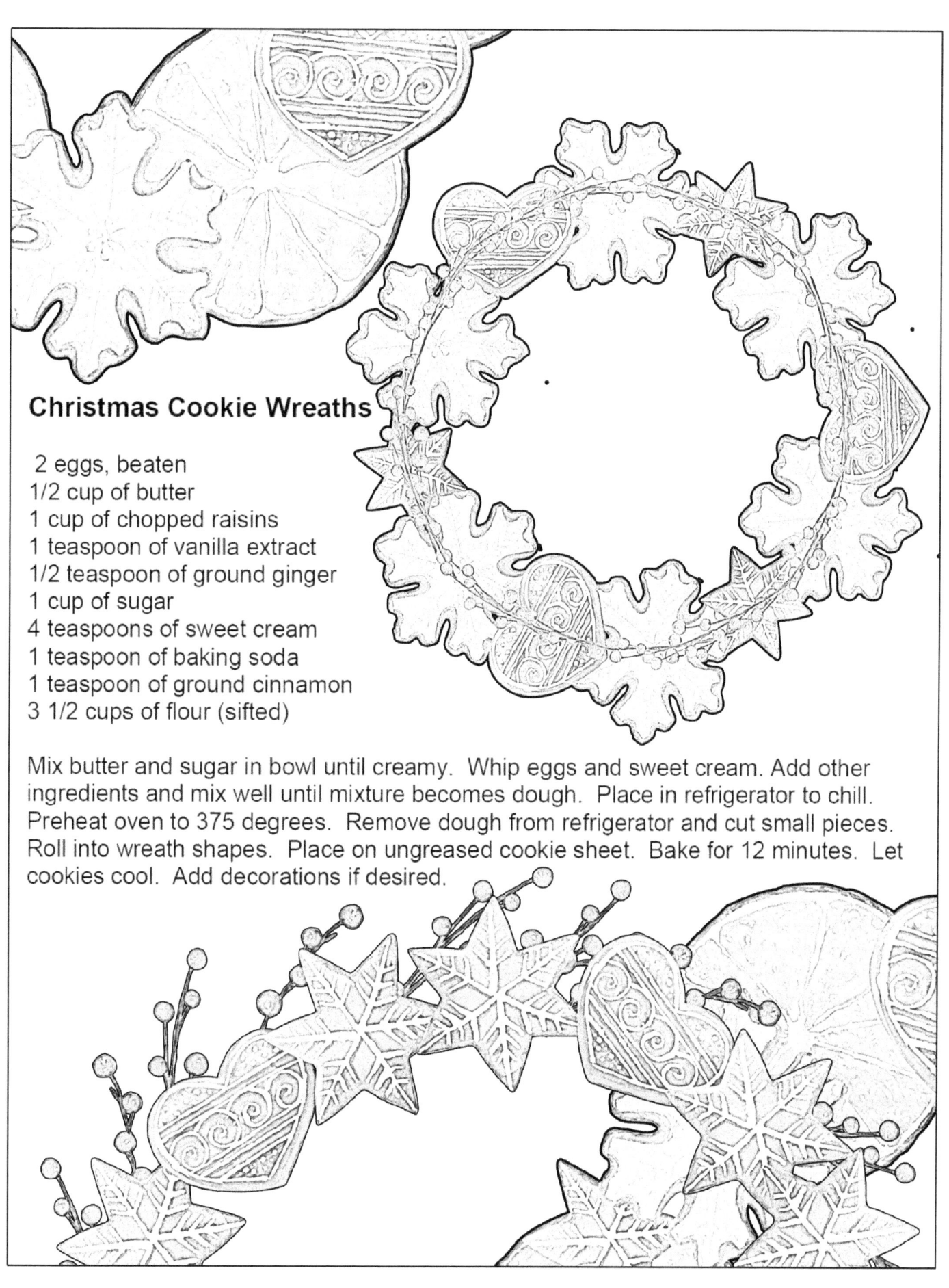

Old Fashioned Butterscotch Cookies

1/2 cup of butter, melted
1 egg
3/4 cup of brown sugar
1 tablespoon of milk
1/2 teaspoon of vanilla extract
1 1/4 cups of flour
1/4 teaspoon of salt
1/4 teaspoon of baking powder

Melt butter and add brown sugar; dissolve well. Add egg and vanilla. Beat well.
Add milk, flour, salt, and baking powder. Mix and drop by teaspoons-full onto a greased cookie sheet one inch apart.
Bake 8 minutes or until light brown at 375F.

Filled Christmas Cookies

For The Dough:

1/2 cup of shortening
1 cup of sugar
1 egg, beaten
1/2 cup of milk
1 teaspoon of vanilla extract
3 1/2 cups of all-purpose flour
1 teaspoon of soda
2 teaspoons of cream of tartar

For The Filling:

1 cup of raisins
1 cup of shredded coconut
1 cup of brown sugar
1/2 cup of water
3 tablespoons of flour
1/2 cup of black walnuts

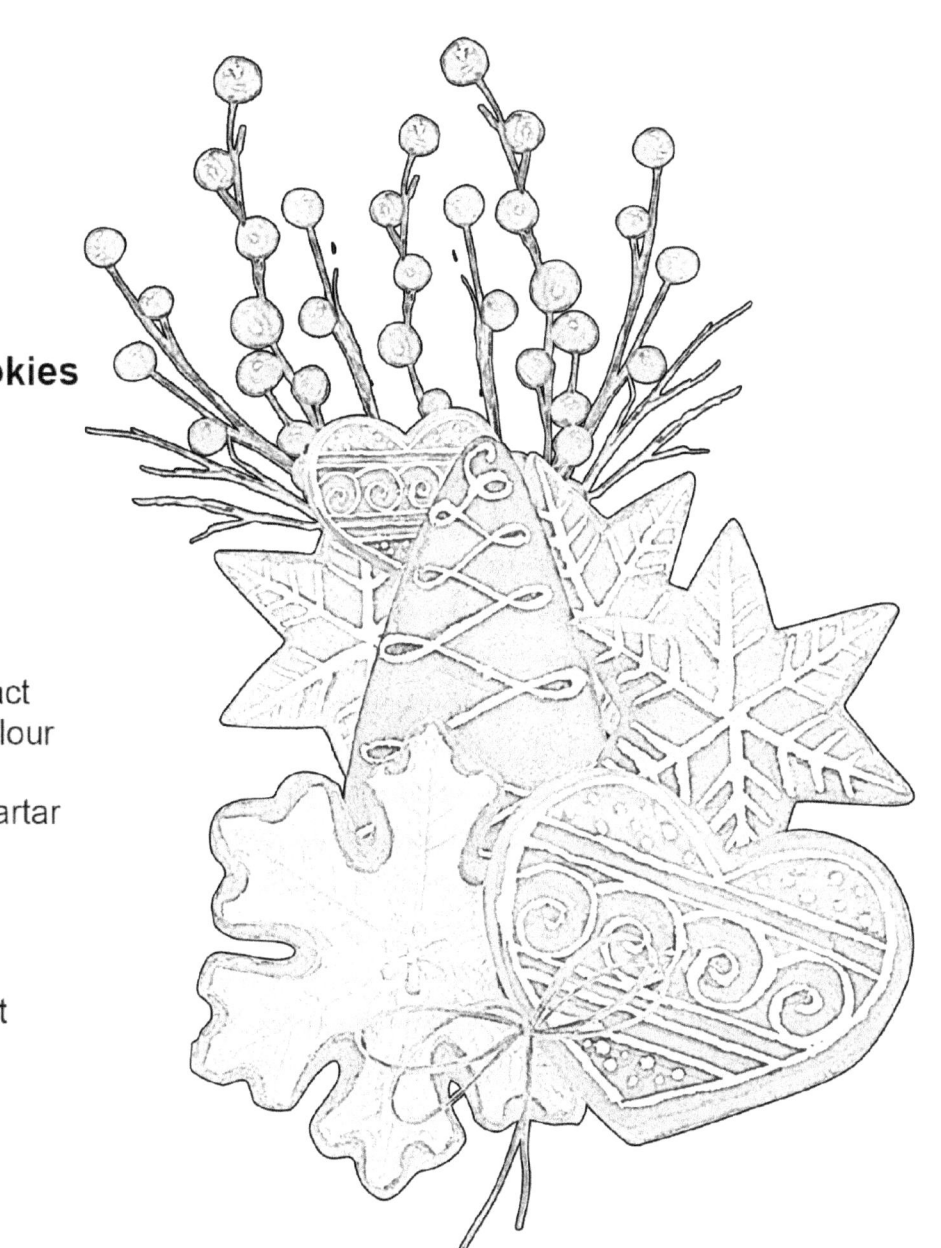

For The Filling:
Mix all ingredients together and cook 5 minutes.

For The Cookies:
Cream shortening and sugar until light and fluffy; stir in egg. Combine milk and vanilla; set aside. Combine flour, soda and cream of tartar; add to creamed mixture alternately with milk mixture, beginning and ending with flour mixture and mixing well after each addition. Roll half of dough on lightly floured board to 1/8 inch thickness, cut with 2 inch round cookie cutters. Place on lightly greased baking sheets; spread 1 teaspoon filling over each. Roll remaining dough to 1/8 inch thickness; cut with 2 inch round cookie cutters and place over filling. Lightly press outer edges together. Bake at 350 degrees for 10 minutes or until lightly browned.

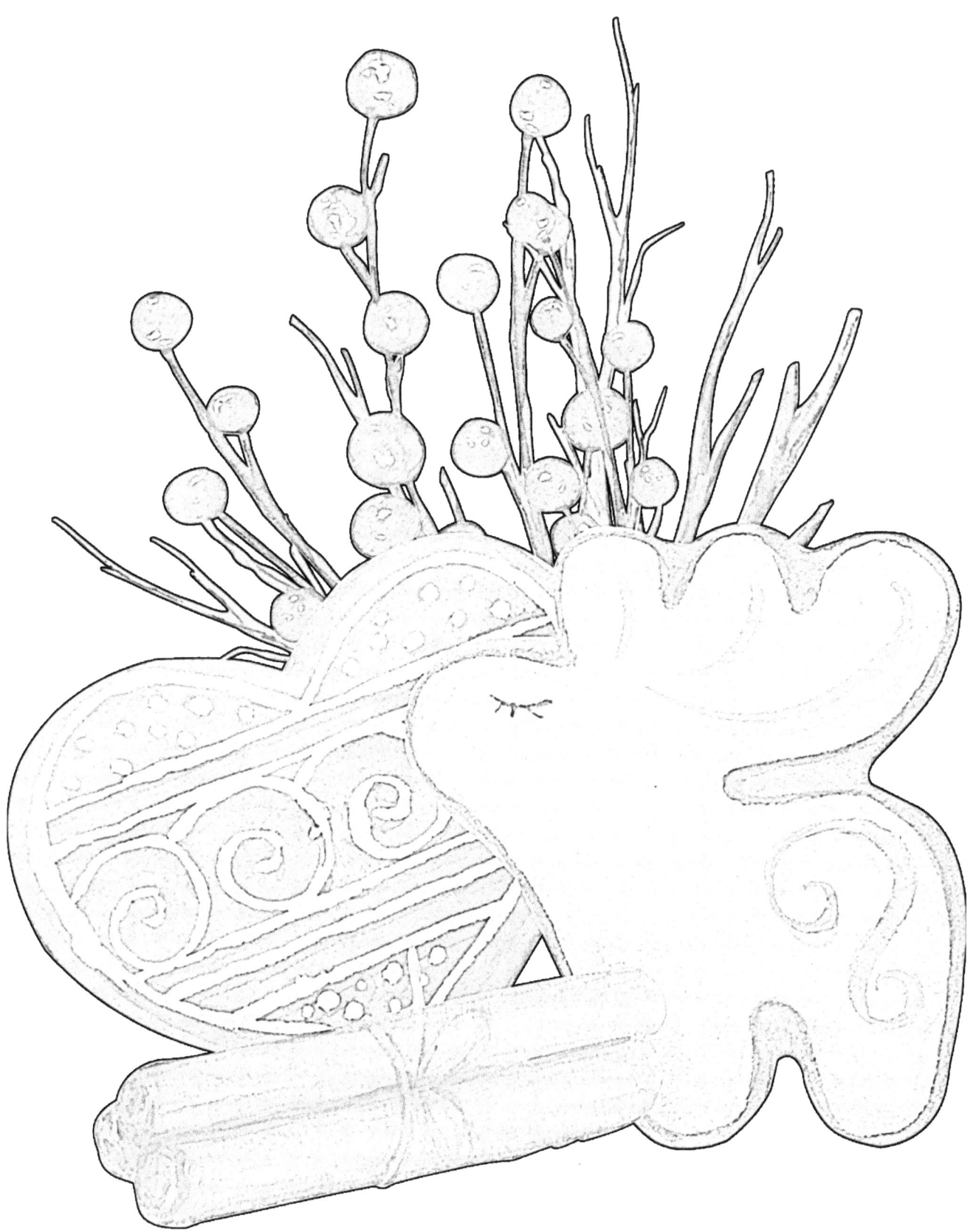

Christmas Cookie Slices

For The Dark Mixture:

3 cups of flour
1 teaspoon of soda
1/4 teaspoon of salt
1/2 teaspoon of ground cinnamon
1 cup of shortening
1 1/2 cups of brown sugar
2 eggs
1 cup of raisins, ground
1 cup of nuts, ground

For The Light Mixture:

2 cups of flour
1/4 teaspoon of salt
1/2 teaspoon of soda
1/2 cup of shortening
3/4 cup of sugar
1 egg
1 teaspoon of vanilla
2 tablespoons of water
1/4 cup of chopped candied cherries

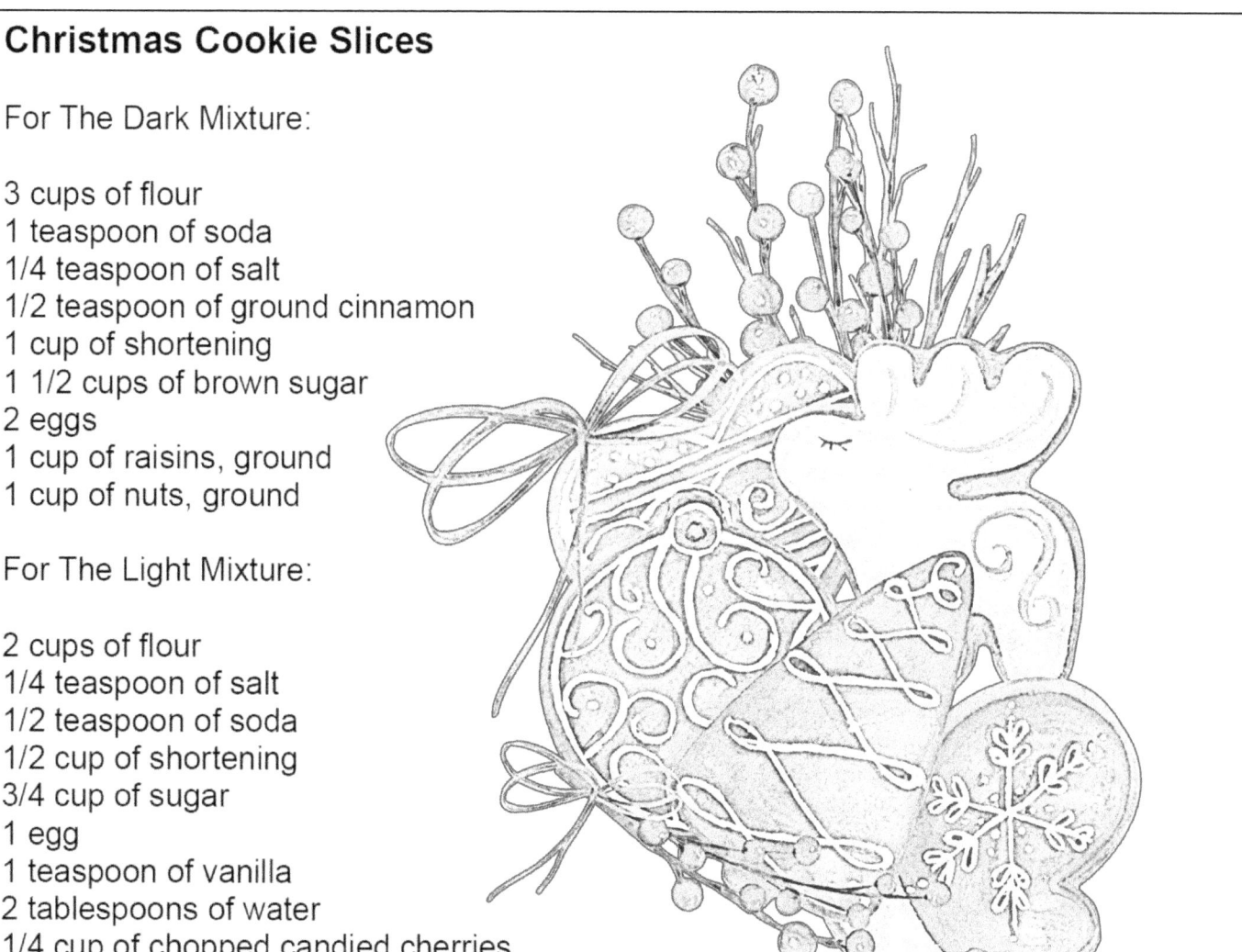

Dark Mixture:
Sift together flour, soda, salt and spices. Cream shortening with brown sugar, add eggs and beat well. Stir in dry ingredients, nuts and raisins.

Light Mixture:
Sift together flour, salt and soda. Cream shortening and sugar, add egg, vanilla and water and mix well. Blend in dry ingredients. Stir in cherries. Pack half of dark mixture into wax paper lined straight-sided pan 10 1/2 x 3 1/2 x 2 1/2 inches. Add all of light dough to make a second layer, top with remaining dark dough. Pack firmly. Refrigerate at least 24 hours. Remove from pan and cut dough lengthwise in half. Then slice in 1/4 inch slices. Bake on ungreased cookie sheet at 400 degrees for 8-10 minutes. Remove immediately from pan.

Butter Cookie Christmas Cutouts

1 cup of butter
1 1/2 cups of sifted powdered sugar
1 egg
1 teaspoon of vanilla
2 1/2 cups of sifted flour
1 teaspoon of cream of tartar
1 teaspoon of baking soda
1/4 teaspoon of salt

Cream butter, add sugar gradually
and cream until fluffy.
 Add unbeaten egg and vanilla; beat we
Sift together dry ingredients; blend into
cream mixture.
Chill dough about an hour.
Roll on well floured pastry board
 to 1/4 inch thickness.
Cut with floured cutter.
Bake on an unbuttered cookie sheet for
6 minutes at 325 degrees.
Yield: 6 dozen cookies.

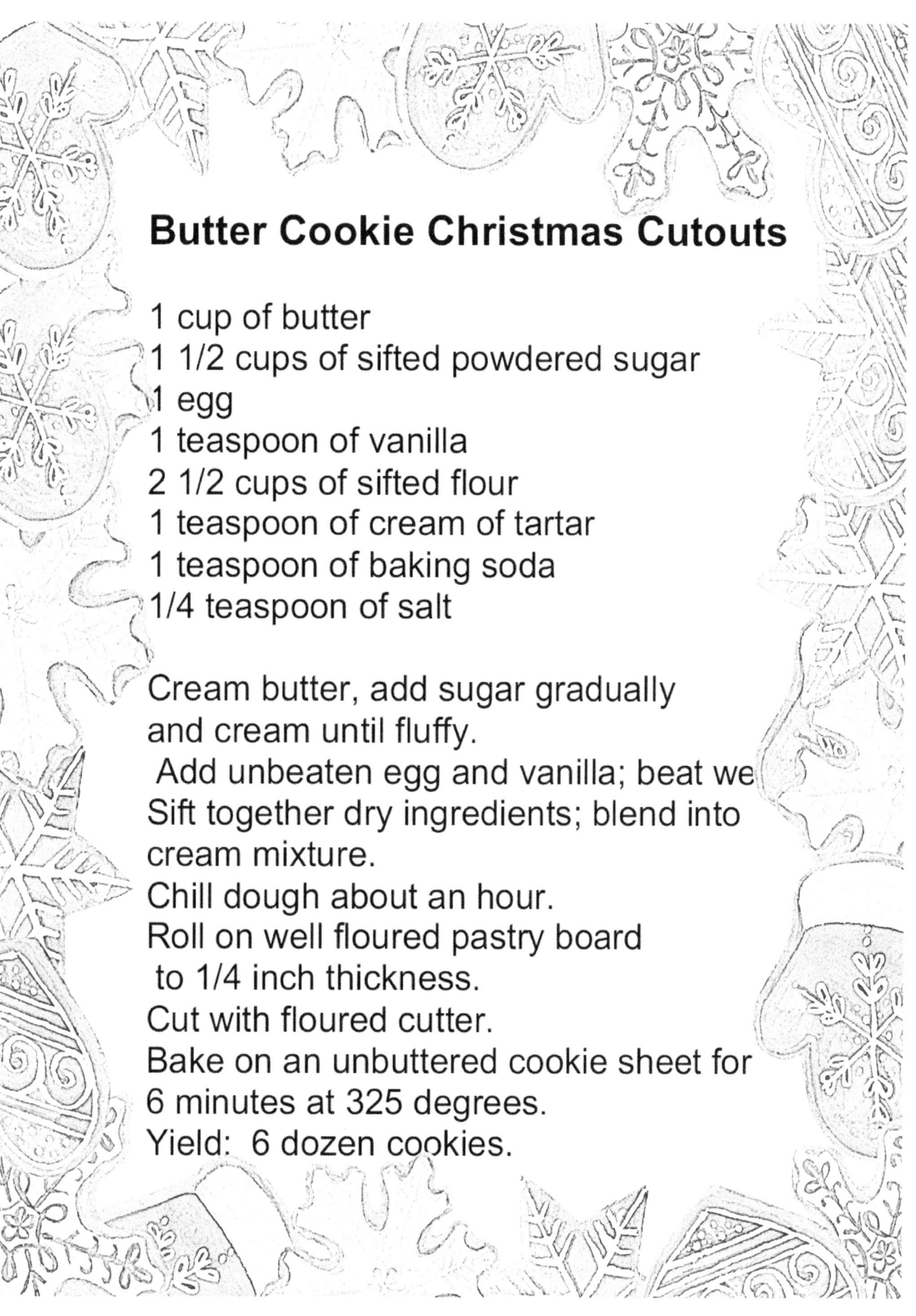

Date Pinwheels

1 lb. of pitted dates, chopped
1/2 cup of water
1/2 cup of sugar

2 1/2 cups of flour
1/2 teaspoon of soda
1/4 teaspoon of salt
3/4 cup of butter or margarine
1/2 cup of firmly packed brown sugar
1/2 cup of sugar
2 eggs, well beaten
1/2 teaspoon of vanilla extract
1 cup of finely chopped nuts

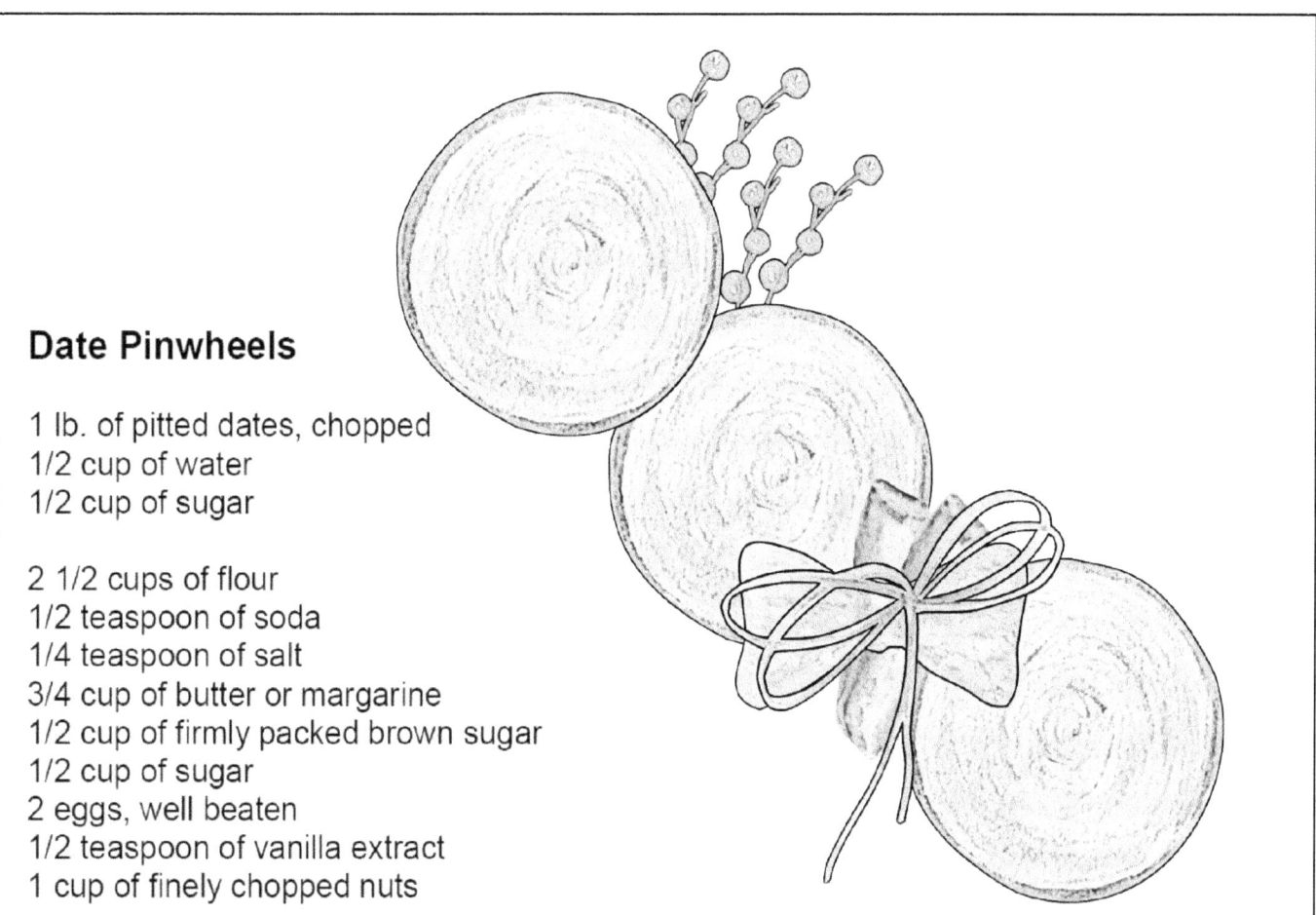

Cook the first three ingredients (dates, water, and sugar) until thick, stirring constantly. Cool. Mix butter, sugars, salt and soda in a separate bowl. Add eggs, vanilla, and flour. Chill dough for 30 minutes. Roll 1/2 of dough out on waxed paper. Spread 1/2 of cooled mixture on the rolled dough. Roll up dough. Slice dough. Bake for seven minutes at 400 degrees.

Peanut Butter Bars

1/2 cup of butter or margarine
1/2 cup of firmly packed brown sugar
1/2 cup of sugar
1 large egg
1 teaspoon of vanilla
1/3 cup of crunchy style peanut butter
1 cup of unbleached flour; sifted
1/2 teaspoon of Baking Soda
1/4 teaspoon of salt
1 cup of quick cooking oats
1 cup of semi-sweet chocolate chips

Cream the butter, brown sugar, and sugar in a mixing bowl until light and fluffy, using an electric mixer at medium speed. Beat in the egg and vanilla. Blend in the peanut butter. Sift the flour, baking soda and salt together. Stir the dry ingredients into the creamed mixture, blending well. Stir in the oats. Spread the mixture in a greased 13 X 9 X 2-inch baking pan. Sprinkle with the chocolate chips. Bake in a 350 degree F. oven for 25 minutes or until done. Cool in the pan on a rack. While still warm drizzle with the vanilla glaze. When cooled, cut into 48 (2 X 1 1/2-inch) bars.

For The Vanilla Glaze:

1/4 cup of confectioners' sugar
1/4 cup of peanut butter
2 tablespoons of butter or margarine
1/4 cup of hot milk
1/2 teaspoon of vanilla

Combine all of the ingredients in a bowl and beat, with an electric mixer set to high speed, until smooth.

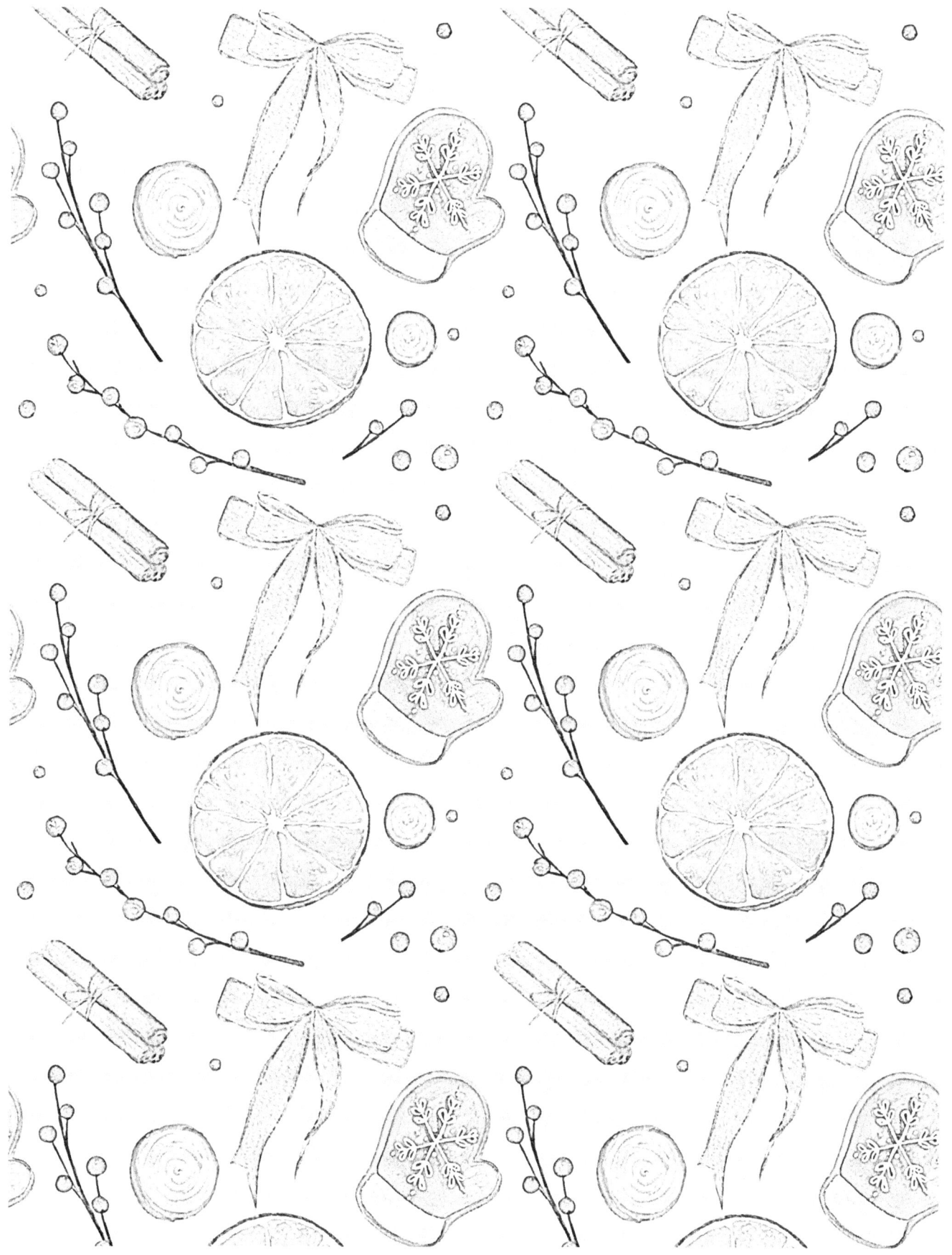

Christmas Surprise Cookies

3/4 cup of shortening
3/4 cup of light brown sugar
1 egg
1 3/4 cups of flour
1 teaspoons of baking soda
1/2 teaspoon of salt
1/2 teaspoon of vanilla extract
3/4 cup of shredded coconut
2 teaspoons of cream of tartar
Any flavor jam or jelly

Cream shortening and sugar together.
Add egg and mix well.
Sift dry ingredients together and add.
Add vanilla, and drop by teaspoons-full onto ungreased cookie sheet.
With your finger or a spoon, make an indentation in the center of the cookie ball and fill with jam or jelly.
Sprinkle coconut over all and bake at 375F for 10-12 min.

Lemon Snow Bars

For The Crust:

1/2 cup of butter
1 cup of flour
1/4 cup of confectioner's sugar

For The Filling:

2 eggs
1 cup of sugar
1/2 teaspoon of baking powder
2 tablespoons of lemon juice
1 teaspoon of grated lemon rind
Confectioner's sugar

Preheat oven to 350 degrees. Combine butter, flour and confectioner's sugar and mix well until mixture clings together. Pat evenly into an ungreased 9 x 9 inch pan. Bake at 350 degrees for 20 minutes or until brown on edges. Beat together eggs, sugar, baking powder, lemon juice and lemon rind (if you don't use rind, add another tablespoon of lemon juice). Pour over partially baked crust. Return to oven and bake 20 minutes longer or until set. Sprinkle with confectioner's sugar. Cool, cut into bars.

Fruited Shortbread Cookies

2 1/2 cups of flour
1 teaspoons of cream of tartar
1 1/2 cups of confectioner's sugar
1 - 9 oz box mincemeat
1 teaspoon of vanilla
1 teaspoon of baking soda
1 cup of utter, softened
1 egg

Preheat oven to 375F.
Combine flour, soda, and cream of tartar.
In a large bowl, beat butter and sugar until fluffy.
Add egg. Stir in vanilla and crumbled mincemeat.
Add dry ingredients. Mix well, batter will be stiff.
Roll into 1 1/4" balls.
Place on ungreased cookie sheet, flatten slightly.
Bake 10-12 minutes or until lightly brown.
Cover with a glaze of confectioner's sugar,
milk and vanilla while still warm.

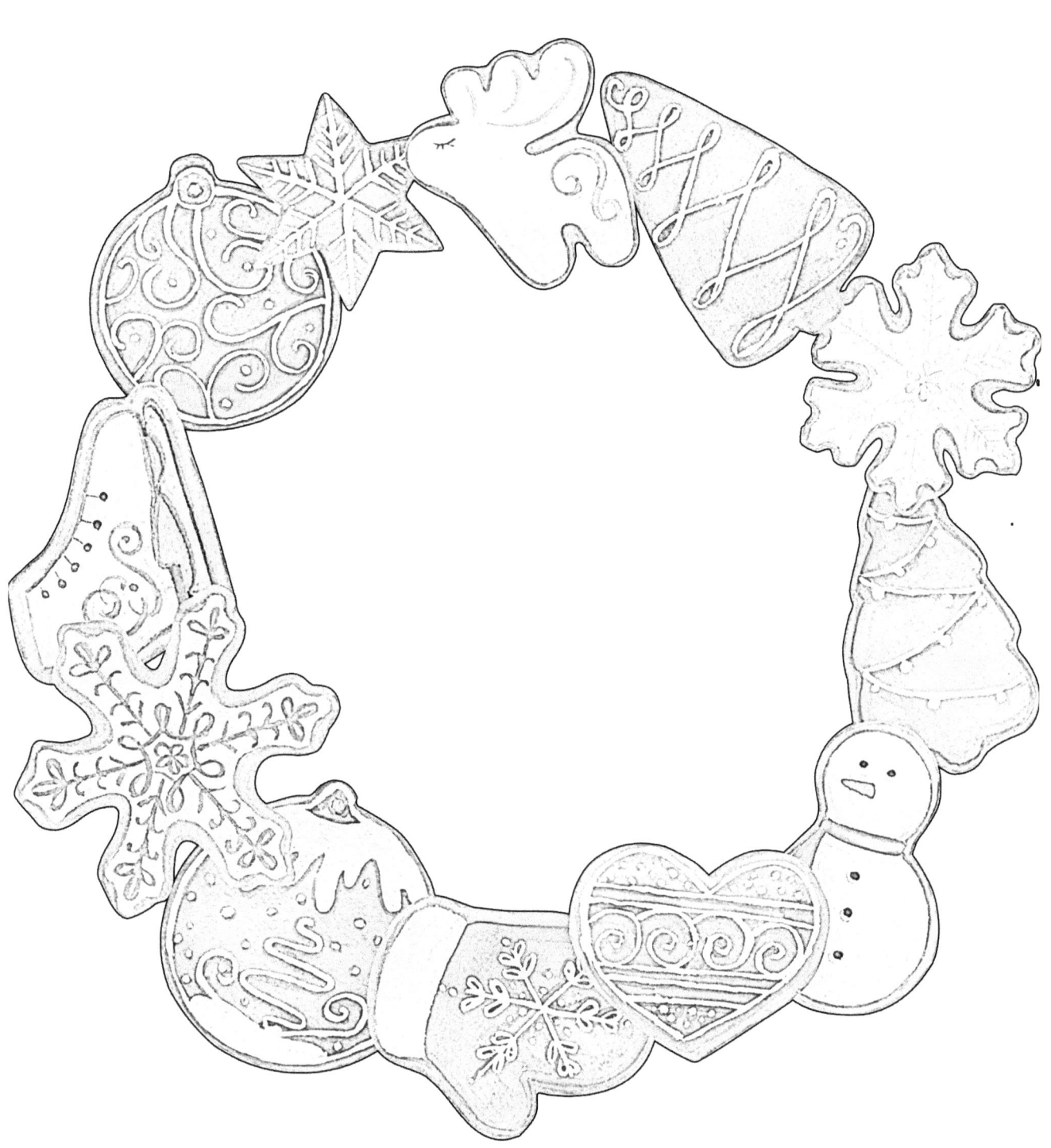

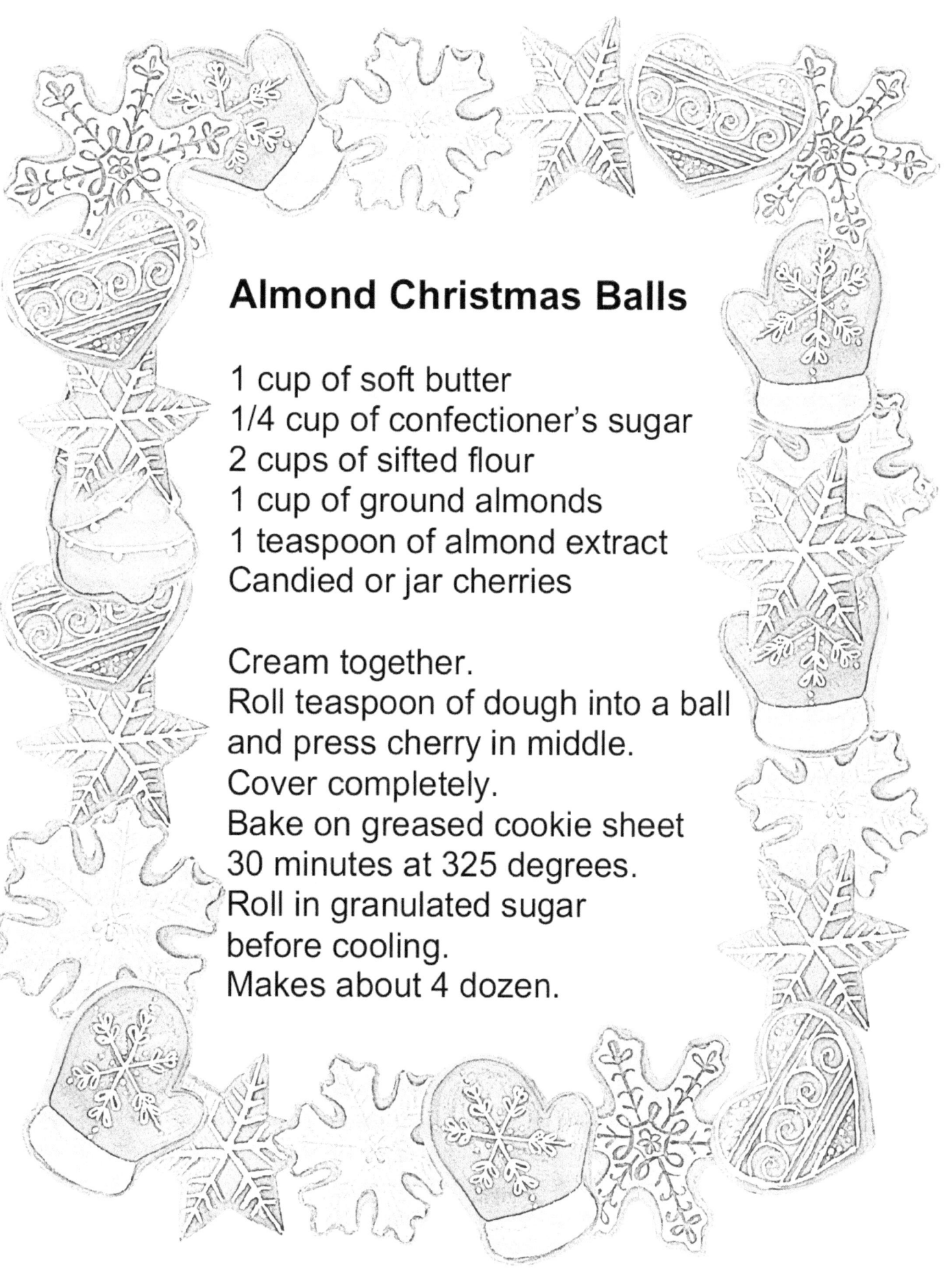

Almond Christmas Balls

1 cup of soft butter
1/4 cup of confectioner's sugar
2 cups of sifted flour
1 cup of ground almonds
1 teaspoon of almond extract
Candied or jar cherries

Cream together.
Roll teaspoon of dough into a ball
and press cherry in middle.
Cover completely.
Bake on greased cookie sheet
30 minutes at 325 degrees.
Roll in granulated sugar
before cooling.
Makes about 4 dozen.

Cinnamon Christmas Logs

1 cup of butter
5 tablespoons of sugar
A dash of salt
2 cups of flour
1 teaspoon of vanilla
1 teaspoon of almond extract
1/4 cup of sugar
1 1/2 tablespoons of ground cinnamon

Mix first 6 ingredients. Roll into 2 inch length logs. Bake at 300 degrees for 15 to 20 minutes. Cool. Roll logs in a sugar and cinnamon mixture.

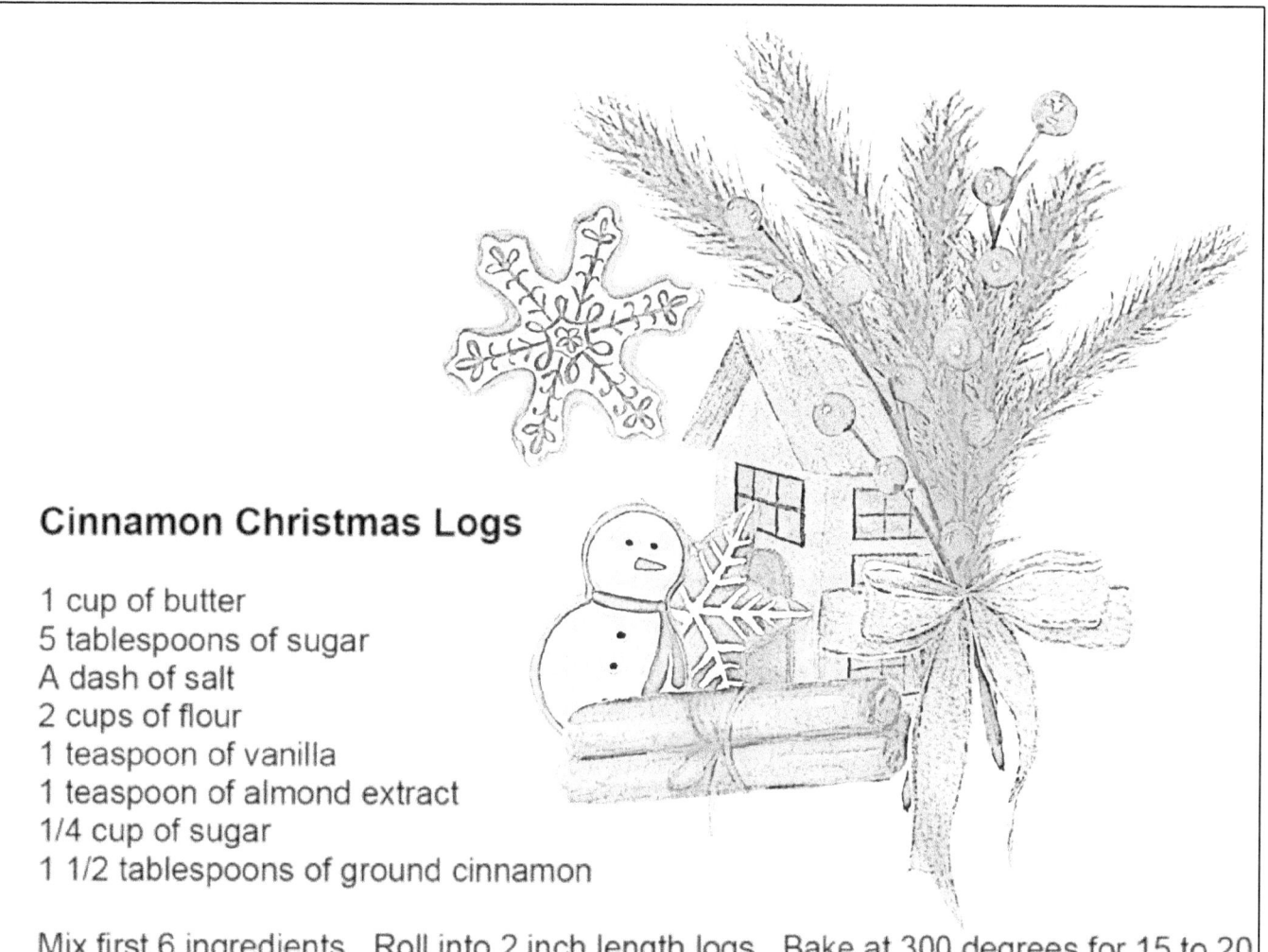

Outrageous Chocolate Chip Cookies

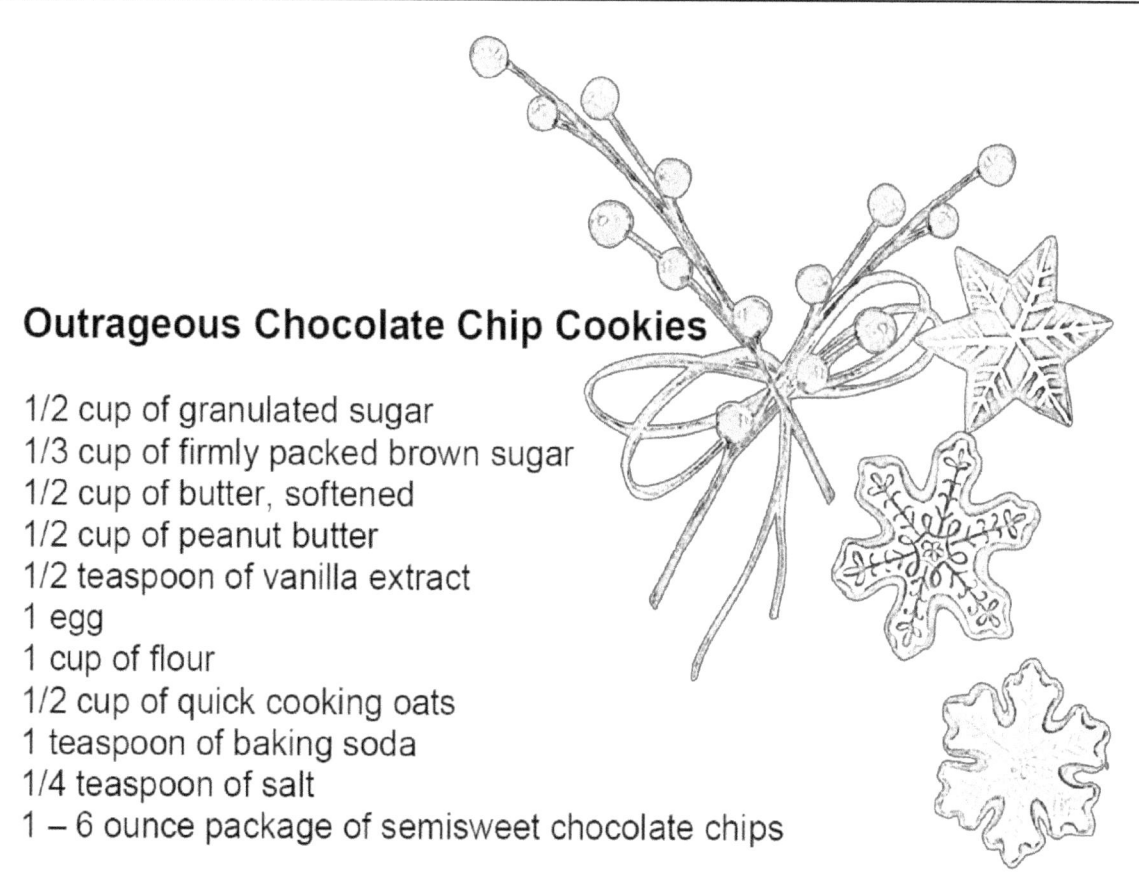

1/2 cup of granulated sugar
1/3 cup of firmly packed brown sugar
1/2 cup of butter, softened
1/2 cup of peanut butter
1/2 teaspoon of vanilla extract
1 egg
1 cup of flour
1/2 cup of quick cooking oats
1 teaspoon of baking soda
1/4 teaspoon of salt
1 – 6 ounce package of semisweet chocolate chips

Heat oven to 350F. Beat sugars, butter, peanut butter, vanilla and egg in a medium bowl, until creamy and well blended. Mix in flour, oats, baking soda and salt. Stir in chocolate chips. Drop dough by rounded teaspoonfuls about 2 inches apart onto ungreased cookie sheet. Bake 10-12 minutes or until light golden brown. Cool 1 minute before removing from cookie sheet.

Christmas Crescent Cookies

1/2 lb. of butter (2 sticks)
2 cups of flour
2 cups of chopped pecans
5 tablespoons of sugar
2 teaspoons of vanilla
1 tablespoon of water
1/2 teaspoon of salt
Powdered Sugar

Cream butter and sugar;
add vanilla and water.
Sift flour and salt, stir into mixture.
Add pecans and mix well.
Shape into size of walnut and
shape into crescent.
Bake slowly at 325 degrees
about 20 minutes.
While warm, roll in powdered sugar.

HAPPY CHRISTMAS TOWN

Coloring book for adults with well known Christmas Lyrics

A grayscale christmas coloring book for adults

Inspire studios

Happy THANKSGIVING Day

An Entertaining Thanksgiving Activity Book

Inspire studios

Gorgeous thanksgiving crafts for kids and decorations for your home!

www.ingramcontent.com/pod-product-compliance
Lightning Source LLC
LaVergne TN
LVHW081612060526
838201LV00054B/2222